THE
POSSIBLE PLEASURES

poems by

Lynn Valente

Finishing Line Press
Georgetown, Kentucky

THE POSSIBLE PLEASURES

Copyright © 2021 by Lynn Valente
ISBN 978-1-64662-688-5 First Edition
All rights reserved under International and Pan-American Copyright Conventions. No part of this book may be reproduced in any manner whatsoever without written permission from the publisher, except in the case of brief quotations embodied in critical articles and reviews.

ACKNOWLEDGMENTS

I would like to thank the following magazines in which some of these poems first appeared: *Jam To-Day* (Don and Judith Stanford, editors), and *Longhouse* (Bob and Susan Arnold, editors).

"Rural Essay" appeared in *Birchsong: Poetry Centered in Vermont*, published by the Blueline Press; and in *Heartbeat of New England*, ed. James Fowler, published by Tiger Moon Press.

"I was a pencil," "Flute Player," and "Literary Love" appeared in 50/50: *Poems & Translations by Womxn over 50*, ed. Ann Davenport, published by QuillsEdge Press.

Publisher: Leah Huete de Maines
Editor: Christen Kincaid
Cover Art: Lynn Valente
Author Photo: Anne Marlantes
Cover Design: Elizabeth Maines McCleavy

Order online: www.finishinglinepress.com
also available on amazon.com

Author inquiries and mail orders:
Finishing Line Press
PO Box 1626
Georgetown, Kentucky 40324
USA

Table of Contents

Centipede 1

Rural Essay 2

Lady Slipper 3

Woodcutter's Autumn 4

We'll Survive Spring 5

The Wind 6

Flute Player 7

UPS Woman 8

Cuernavaca 9

Ozone 10

Giant Steps 11

Glutton 12

Mother's Anger 13

I was a pencil 14

Literary Love 15

The very edge 16

Nothing stirs 17

Out skiing alone 18

A Small One 19

In the Hospital Parking Lot 20

First Minute / Last Minute 21

Centipede

First thing in the a.m.
I step up to my writing station
wishing a poem
would come quick and whole

so I pick a bunch of paper
from the box
and what jumps out
not a poem but

quick and whole
a centipede frantic
I shake the box

it hits the floor
and disappears beneath a board

like a poem   it races my heart

Rural Essay

He is with us on furlough from a flat,
bleached, hard place.
                              "But
don't you get blind sometimes
to beauty?" The starving man
doesn't want to lose his craving
for food.

Listen, mountains seem like food
only until you say
I live here. Then they keep feeding you
the way air feeds you. You don't
consume this place. Think of marriage
to a person with a beautiful face.
His beauty will continue to strike you
often, at odd times, but

if you're to have a life together,
you can't stand around and gape
in wonder more than a few hundred
times a day.

Lady Slipper

The best way to love her
is leave her alone

The head flies apart
if you sigh "But I..."

Even you
may not take this shoe

and search the world
for a perfect fit

She is already chosen
to walk alone

to occupy
the long green throne

If you care, leave her

Don't say where you've seen her

Woodcutter's Autumn

Geese above
barking like dogs
open the gate
to our dark fence
and let in some thoughts
we put away for good—

of summer, that tourist
who took off fast
in his big car
and never paid taxes.
We'll be paying now—

Who let in these thoughts?

From carrying them home
my arms will ache
all winter.

We'll Survive Spring

We fight. I storm out
to watch the sky,
high bright
stars and wisp of moon.
Cool enough still
to keep flies from biting.
They nip a bit,
like the breeze

Road's quiet—all the cars
have long gone home.
Only quiet
should be rising
from the beaver pond:
water's low,
their entranceway
exposed. But comes

the echoing
slap!
of beaver tail

I have to open the door
and tell you that

The Wind

Constant suitor
of many gifts
and big hands

who improvises
a love song quick
across the trees

his tongue turning
from gentle to rough,
trying to swallow me up

and down—
blithe, urgent
undeniable

still he keeps
trying to explain
his hesitation

changes of direction,
endless variations
on why

he just
can't
settle down

his big mouth!—
saying everything
that comes into his head

Flute Player

Spotlight on her fingers and their tiny gestures

Invisible targets for her breath
mounted round the room

tilted princess   wooden door   bamboo shadow

Audience drowning in polite water

Mouthpiece warm against her chin

Audience cuts loose from gravity, floats up
toward the ceiling

Her breath now

must hold them there

UPS Woman

She stands behind the judgment table
magic tape in hand, leaning forward
to see what you bring

Only if your boxes are firm,
free of rattles and useless string
will she agree to let you on:

say quick "what's in 'em?"

Brown-green trucks, perfectly loaded
go shooting from her eyes
in all directions

Cuernavaca

Every Wednesday was market day
time to go and see
the Aztecs who wound down the mountain
as they had done for hundreds of years

time to go and see
the designs that each village wove
as they had done for hundreds of years
calling themselves not Aztec

the designs that each village wove
like maps in color
calling themselves not Aztec
but bearing many flags to market

maps in color
invisible on their faces
bearing many flags to market
protecting the stories and crops they grew

invisible on their faces
maps in color
protecting the stories and crops they grew
no longer using the ancient words

an explosion of color
every Wednesday was market day
still using the ancient words
the Aztecs wound down the mountain

Ozone

On the front stoop we discussed books, religion, music,
and the end of the world.

The nights were warm and sometimes the glow
from the stores downtown didn't blot out the moon.

Out there in the wildest thunderstorm,
you were explaining the smell of ozone
as I was inhaling you—

The storm centered over us.
We left the overhang of roof

to stand in the street, get soaked
and take the ozone.

My mother stood in the doorway,
a box of sleepless nights under her arm
and begged me to return—

Though the roof kept her dry,
she had already begun shrinking.

Giant Steps

The summer they landed on the moon
was the same summer I struggled up
to escape from what had become
a cocoon, though equipped
with tv, telephone, windows.

But I had grown so
that the pale walls were pushing in.
Yet they seemed thin as paper.
Why was escape as impossible as the moon
used to be? I could see I was taller
than my parents. I suspected
they could hear, through paper walls
my wings beating
on certain nights selected by God
and my boyfriend. How could they not
hear me murmur his name? Still
they acted the same, pretended
I was good and quiet and small
as ever. They refused to watch me,
I refused to watch tv.

It droned on—
a comfort, even when the screen
showed only rock and crater. Surely
(as they secured the lock) I would not
actually leave until later?

Glutton

She deprives herself
of the pleasure
of hunger.

All thoughts and words
other than *food*
constitute

a foreign taste
from which she abstains,
forming no sentence

but the one
(pain, plain)
she serves herself.

Mother's Anger

She calls—
we have fallen
too far from the tree.
She is pulling in
all her little apples:
the phone wire
spirals
like disappointment.

Our skins are bright red
yet far too rough.
She frowns at the frost marks,
the death and divorce marks.
She cries, and her sorrow
is sharper than teeth.
Soon she'll bite down
to the tiny poison seeds.

I was a pencil

I was a pencil for Halloween.
First I grew my head to a point
of weighty darkness
yet persisted in holding up
the wooden mask protruding
from the top of my gown.
My gown was gold and orange
painted onto flesh
and embossed
with my number,
nationality
and the finest 2-word poem I'd ever heard:

      Venus
      Velvet

In the moonless night
I ate my candy on the run
from house to house

since I had no baggage
unlike my sisters,
the witch and the princess.

Literary Love

I tried to get you to love me
by mouthing some words from a book

I didn't know
you'd picked up my book, let it
fall open to just that page
on which she is trying to get him—

Those words happened to become
available to me
as in learning a foreign
language: to get them
to pass you salt at the table,
say *these words*. But now
you think I'm a literary
person, a literary love

and I am ashamed
as if you had undressed me
and found my clothes
paper
my heart
ink
my skin
more paper
with nothing of interest
to read there
my whole body
a pencil
trying
to write you down

The very edge

While we love
I leave a part of

myself aside—I cleave
in two.

The cold, gray, lone wife
I push to the very edge of the bed

and would bid her
fall off

if I could spare
the attention.

Nothing stirs

Nothing stirs until I claim stairs, light
switch, faucet and stove.
Even if I've come through a night of boxing
demons and stars, a night of
split decisions, still I claim this hour
as my prize—its scent of emptiness,
its sky of deliberation.

I like the way
I am small at this hour, the way
there is no one to raise an eyebrow
if I sit long enough at my teacup
for the moon to come drown there.
I'm still slippery
with sleep—nothing sticks
to me. Even my tools and marble
lie still on the bench—in this light
they don't gleam with expectation.

Miss this hour and I keep on missing
all day. I don't have
your energy, your dash from bed to table
to road to port, straight out across
the water. I love to watch
you take off, your dark blur, but now
alone in the blue kitchen,
I guard carefully
the last stillness. I will not
wake you, or bring you down
here, where nothing
stirs.

Out Skiing Alone

This washboard snow
knows nothing of my clumsiness: how I think I hurt you
when I don't, how I hurt you sometimes
never knowing.

The land must think
I am a deer—this flying
even works uphill. I've never stayed up
so long before on folding, bending
earth. For this one moment
I don't need to figure out
anything. The land
must think.

One ski leaps out behind me, the other
guides forward a mile to the pond.
In the sound of my own skis
sweeping, I hear
your voice call me, my secret
name. This loving
even works uphill.

A Small One

He knows
    how to take

comfort
    from me

He reaches,
    he grabs

as much
    as he needs

He needs,
    he takes—

I follow
    his lead:

at night
    I walk him

slowly
    to sleep

The spicy
    comfort

of his warm
    weight

(a life
    jacket)

encircles
    me

In the Hospital Parking Lot

I leaned my head
against the steering wheel
and cried, not caring
how it looked

The car stood still, the earth
was turning. I leaned
into the staring wail.
I touched
against the story wall.
There was no will.
The car stood still.

In official waiting rooms
those who cared
about how it looked
came to see me cry

but all my grief was left
outside, in the rusting car
where plastic seats
would not absorb it
in the calm way of these
gray shoulders.

First Minute / Last Minute

1.
I want to study the light
particle by particle,
but it all comes
crashing at once
in a wave,
a strong

undertow here
uncertain shapes
to guide me

I carry the ancient
odor of salt
up a wide soft beach
to find the sun
my father's face

brimming with all
he must wait
to show me

2.
Darkness closes
in from the edge
like wearing a hat
too large, it keeps
slipping
slipping down

The dizzy planet
that is my room
slows gradually

Those bending over me
open their mouths
but the air
has slowed so much
I hear

only a roar
like surf
pounding

Lynn Valente was born in Brooklyn and grew up on Long Island. She moved to Vermont to study at Marlboro College and at the School for International Training. She is retired from teaching Spanish in a small rural high school. She has published both her own work and translations from Spanish in various publications. She still lives in Vermont, where she is an avid skier, hiker, and amateur musician.

www.ingramcontent.com/pod-product-compliance
Lightning Source LLC
LaVergne TN
LVHW041524070426
835507LV00012B/1802